MASS FOR FIVE VOICES

BY

WILLIAM BYRD

EDITED AND ARRANGED FOR MODERN USE BY

HENRY WASHINGTON

Duration of performance 30 minutes

CHESTER MUSIC

PREFACE

THIS new transcription of Byrd's Masses for three, four and five voices respectively has been prepared mainly to meet the demand for a practical choir edition. Although these masterpieces of Tudor polyphony have long been familiar through earlier transcriptions by Rimbault, Rockstro, Barclay Squire, Terry and Fellowes a few textual uncertainties have persisted. I have therefore used the occasion to make a definitive score by reference to the set of original part-books in the British Museum. Thus for the first time in a separate publication of these works any editorial suggestions are readily distinguishable from the original text. Byrd's own accidentals are printed in the normal position, i.e. to the left of the note affected while other accidentals, added for whatever reason, appear in small type above the note. A system of regular barring has been applied having regard to the fact that the training and equipment of the present-day chorister bear little relation to those of his sixteenth-century counterpart. Experience has shown that any visual advantage to the rhythmic flow derived from irregular barring is diminished in practice by difficulties of counting and place-finding.

The music text is here set out unencumbered with arbitrary marks of expression. In this way the director is free to insert such guides to performance as he thinks expedient, and singers are spared the confusion induced by his insistence on, say, a *pianissimo* reading when the edited score demands a contrary effect. A suggested scheme of interpretation is incorporated in the *reductio partiturae*. The sign ⸓, a short vertical stroke placed above or below a note, is freely used in this edition with the twofold object of defending verbal rhythm against the accentual power associated with the modern bar-line, and of defining the true agogic rhythm where an original long note has been replaced by two tied notes of shorter duration. Sixteenth-century note-values have been halved to accord with later acceptance of the crotchet as the normal unit of time. The slur is used solely to denote a ligature. The present Mass for Five Voices is transposed down a tone from the original with advantage to all parts in the average SATTB complement.

No exact date can be assigned either to the composition or to the publication of the three Masses. The few surviving exemplars were discovered without title-page or any sort of pre-fatory matter. As long ago as 1913 the late H. B. Collins, my revered tutor, called attention to Byrd's use of the barred semi-circle, ₵, for the five-part Mass and the unbarred semi-circle, C, for the other two. For many years past an erroneous statement relating to this fact has been widely circulated and often repeated*. It is to the effect that Byrd's publications from 1605 to 1611 were printed under the barred semi-circle, ₵, and that Mr. Collins drew from this the inference that the five-part Mass was a *late* composition. The truth is precisely the opposite. Byrd used the barred semi-circle for his publications from 1575 to 1591 and the unbarred semi-circle from 1605 to 1611. Mr. Collins actually suggested, for what it was worth, that the five-part Mass was therefore an *early* work dating from the time of the *Cantiones Sacrae* whereas the three and four-part Masses belonged to a much later period. In fact a transcript of the three-part Mass is to be found in Baldwin's manuscript dated 1603; and if, as seems almost certain, the Masses were printed by Thomas East the four-part Mass must have been finished by 1608; East died before January 17th, 1609. It may be presumed that the three Masses were published together—albeit surreptitiously—in the year 1610; for the British Museum set is not the only one to have been found interleaved with Redmer's 1610 impression of the Second Book of *Gradualia*.

HENRY WASHINGTON

THE ORATORY,
LONDON,
January, 1960

*William Byrd by E. H. Fellowes. 1923, 1936, 1948. O.U.P. and *Tudor Church Music*, Vol. IX, 1928.

MASS FOR FIVE VOICES

WILLIAM BYRD
Edited by
HENRY WASHINGTON

KYRIE

GLORIA

CREDO

SANCTUS

BENEDICTUS

AGNUS DEI